Get ready to hear your kids say, "Wow! I didn't know that!" as they dive into this fun, informative, question-answering series of books! Students—and teachers and parents—will learn things about the world around them that they never knew before!

This approach to education seeks to promote an interest in learning by answering questions kids have always wondered about. When books answer questions that kids already want to know the answers to, kids love to read those books, fostering a love for reading and learning, the true keys to lifelong education.

Colorful graphics are labeled and explained to connect with visual learners, while in-depth explanations of each subject will connect with those who prefer reading or listening as their learning style.

This educational series makes learning fun through many levels of interaction. The in-depth information combined with fantastic illustrations promote learning and retention, while question and answer boxes reinforce the subject matter to promote higher order thinking.

Teachers and parents love this series because it engages young people, sparking an interest and desire in learning. It doesn't feel like work to learn about a new subject with books this interactive and interesting.

This set of books will be an addition to your home or classroom library that everyone will enjoy. And, before you know it, you, too, will be saying, "Wow! I didn't know that!"

"People cannot learn by having information pressed into their brains. Knowledge has to be sucked into the brain, not pushed in. First, one must create a state of mind that craves knowledge, interest, and wonder. You can teach only by creating an urge to know." - Victor Weisskopf

Contents under license from Aladdin Books Ltd.

Flowerpot Press
142 2nd Avenue North
Franklin, TN 37064

Flowerpot Press is a division of Kamalu, LLC,
Franklin, TN, U.S.A.,
and Mitso Media, Inc., Oakville, ON, Canada.

ISBN 978-1-77093-773-4

Concept, editorial, and design by
David West Children's Books

Designer:
Simon Morse

Illustrators:
Gerald Witcomb and Don Simpson - Spec Arts
Jo Moore

American Edition Editor:
Johannah Gilman Paiva

American Redesign:
Jonas Fearon Bell

Printed in China.

All rights reserved.

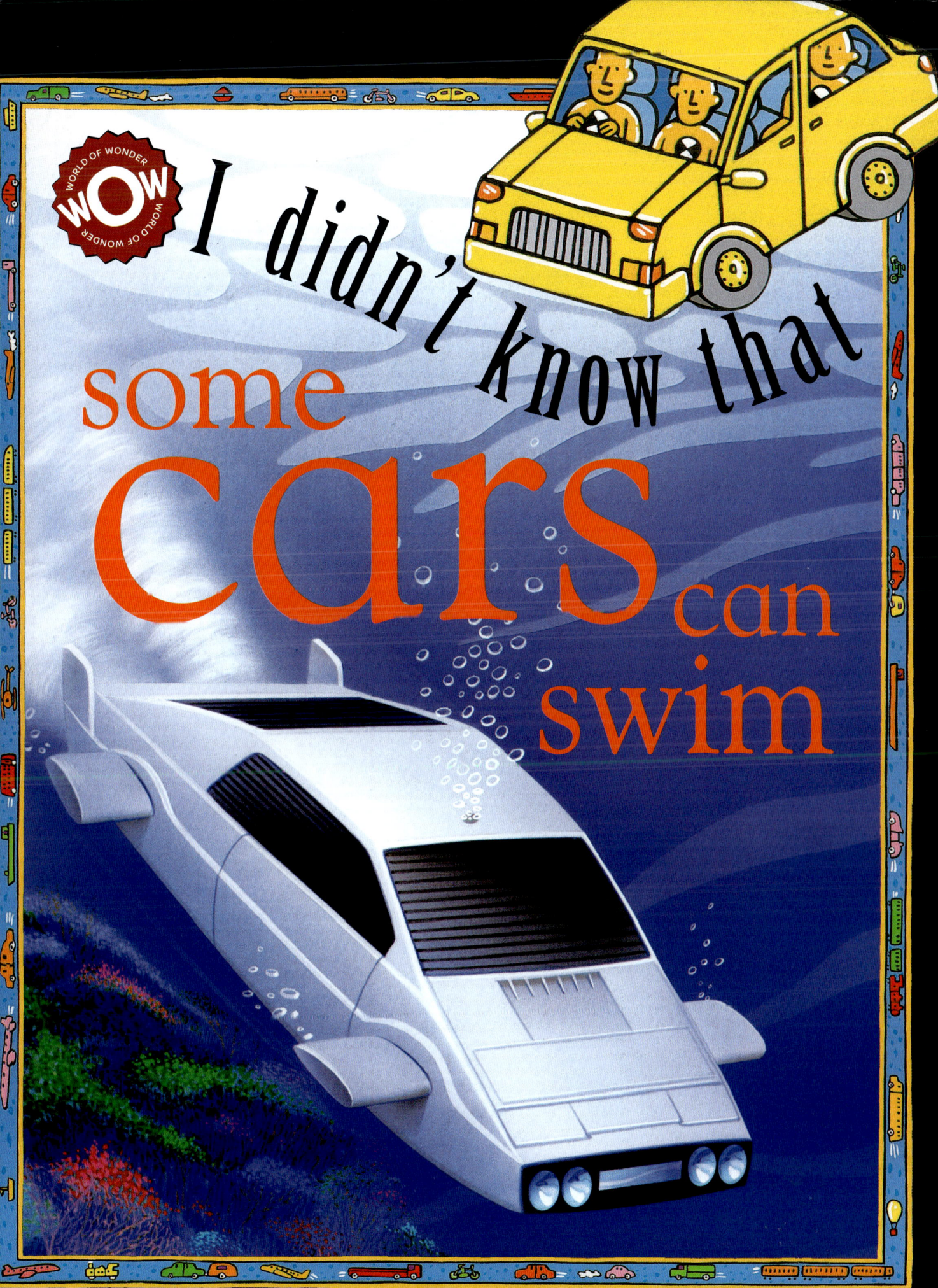

I didn't know that

introduction 5

the first cars had three wheels 6

cars are powered by explosions 8

robots build cars 10

the best car in the world is a ghost 12

a T-bird is a car 14

dummies test cars 16

some cars have wings 18

some cars need parachutes 20

a car can go faster than sound 22

some cars can swim 24

some cars have two engines 26

cars in the future will have brains 28

glossary 30

index 32

Introduction

Did you know some cars can cross rivers? That in 1920, half of the world's cars were exactly the same model? That Formula One crews can change four tires in seconds?

Discover for yourself amazing facts about cars, from the very earliest models that went at walking pace to today's record breakers that go faster than the speed of sound.

Watch for this symbol, which means there is a fun project for you to try.

True or False? Watch for this symbol and try to answer the question before reading on for the answer.

! Don't forget to check the borders for extra amazing facts.

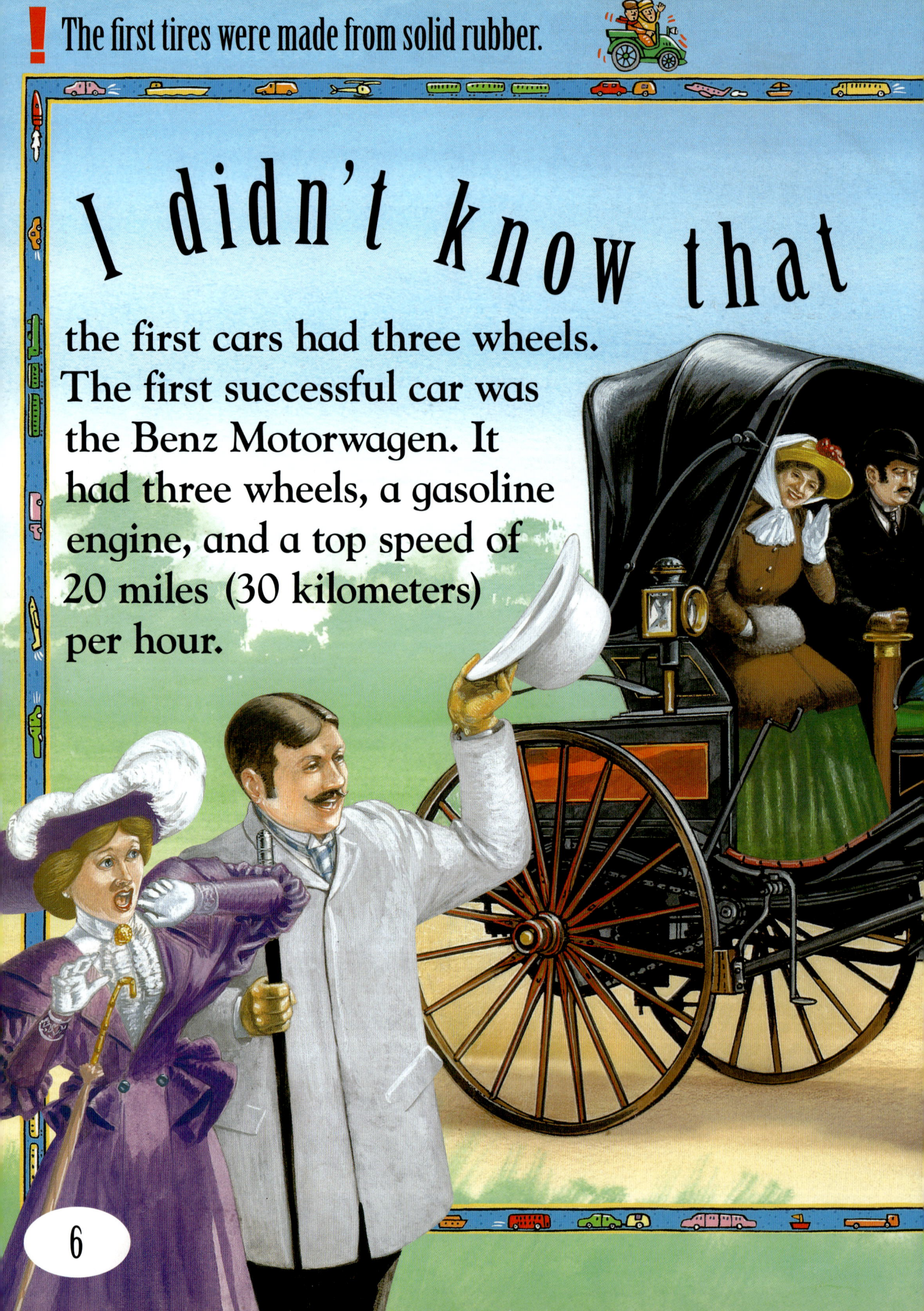

! The first tires were made from solid rubber.

I didn't know that

the first cars had three wheels. The first successful car was the Benz Motorwagen. It had three wheels, a gasoline engine, and a top speed of 20 miles (30 kilometers) per hour.

6

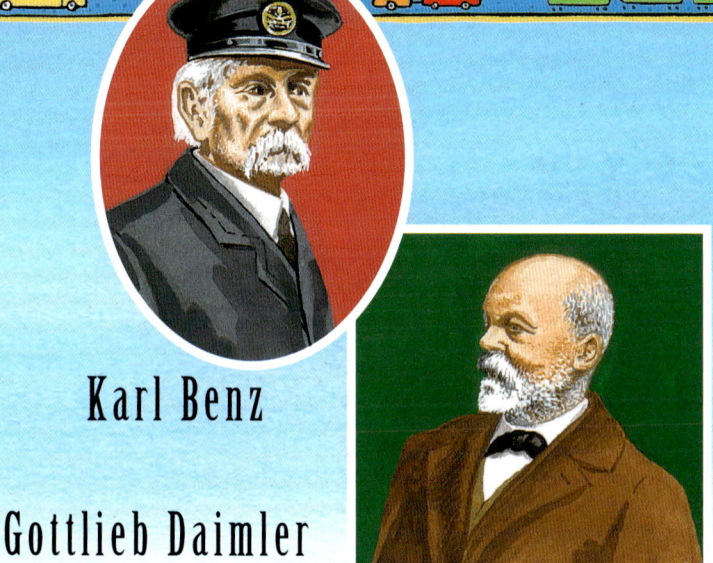

Karl Benz

Gottlieb Daimler

The Bordino Steam Carriage of 1854 replaced horses with steam power. It was very heavy and cumbersome, and slower than traveling by train. The gasoline engine made such "horseless carriages" look old-fashioned.

Karl Benz and Gottlieb Daimler built the Motorwagen in Munnheim, Germany, in 1886. Do you recognize their names?

 **True or False?**
Early cars had no speed limit.

Answer: **False.** The 1865 British law said that cars must follow a man with a red flag at less than 4 miles (6.5 kilometers) per hour.

 Since early cars were open, coats and hats were essential!

! Some cars use engines from airplanes!

I didn't know that

cars are powered by explosions. Gasoline explodes inside a car's engine. The force created by the explosion pushes the pistons, which turn the wheels of the car.

Can you find the car keys?

An internal combustion engine works in four stages, which make up one cycle:
1. Gasoline and air mixture are sucked into cylinder.
2. Mixture is compressed.
3. Spark causes explosion.
4. Waste gases are expelled.

True or False?
All cars have engines under the hood.

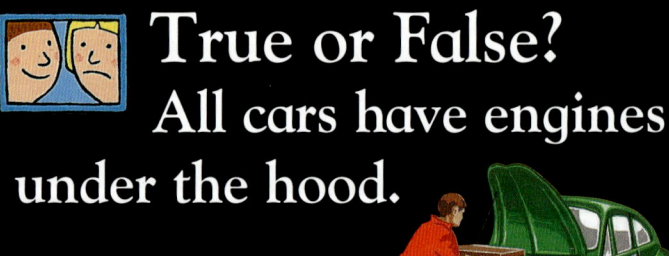

Answer: False. Some, such as the Volkswagen Beetle and the Fiat Seicento, have the engine in the trunk! Under the hood, there is space for luggage.

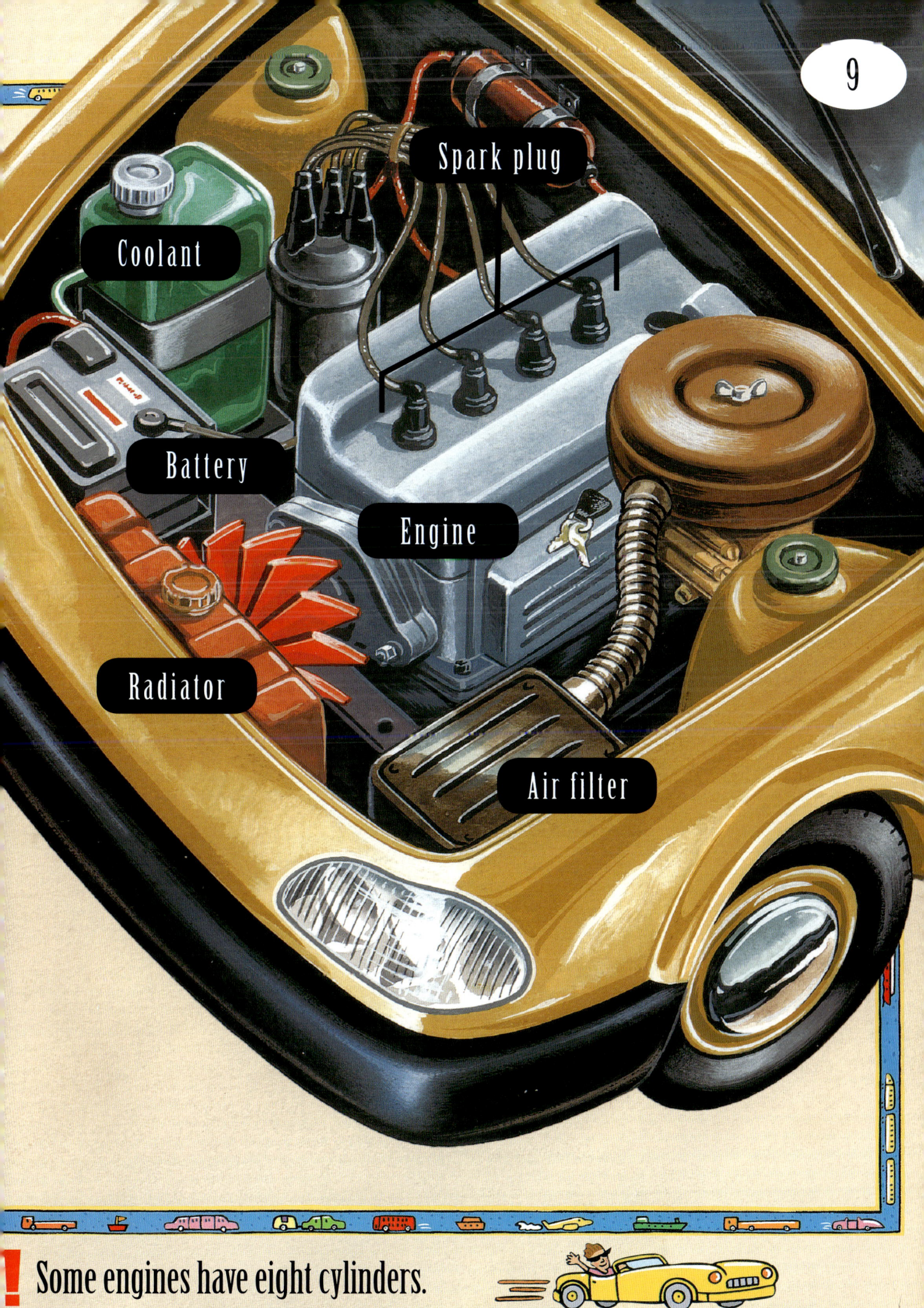

Some engines have eight cylinders.

! About 50 million new cars are made every year.

I didn't know that

robots build cars. Modern cars are built quickly and accurately by robots, each with its own task. Robots can work in conditions that are too hot, noisy, or dangerous for humans.

The Model-T Ford was the world's first ever mass-produced car. In 1914, Henry Ford invented the production line for building cars.

Today, modern cars are designed using computers. Designers can easily see what the finished car will look like. Then, a life-sized clay model of the car is tested in a wind tunnel for aerodynamic properties.

10

Air travels more easily over smooth surfaces than blunt ones. Cover one car with an L-shaped strip of cardstock and the other with a smooth, curved strip. Roll both cars down a slope, blowing a hair drier set on cold at them. Which one wins and why?

All the cars in the world, end-to-end, would go around the world 34 times.

! The longest limousine is over 98 feet (30 meters) long!

I didn't know that

the best car in the world is a ghost. The Rolls Royce Silver Ghost is renowned for its superb engine and stylish looks. Some people consider it to be the best car in the world.

The stylish 1935 Auburn Speedster was perfect for cruising around glamorous Hollywood. Each car came with a plaque certifying that it had been driven at over 99 miles (160 kilometers) per hour by racing driver Ab Jenkins.

The most expensive car ever was the enormous Bugatti Royale. It was 22 feet (6.7 meters) long! Only six of them were ever made. In 1990, a Royale was sold at an auction for $15 million.

One of the greatest Grand Prix cars of all time was the 1937 Mercedes W125. With the help of two enormous superchargers, it reached speeds of almost 199 miles (320 kilometers) per hour!

I didn't know that

a T-bird is a car. In the 1950s, Ford offered a $250 suit to whoever named their sporty new car. Thunderbird (an Australian bird), or "T-bird" for short, was the winner.

Can you find the three cola bottles?

As later Thunderbirds got bigger, the Ford Company built the Mustang—a smaller sports car, very popular with young Americans. Over a million were sold in three years.

The Volkswagen Beetle is the best-selling car ever. Over 20 million have been sold! They were designed and built in Germany in the 1930s to boost the German economy and provide a cheap, reliable "people's car."

The Mini was designed in the 1950s as a cheap and efficient car for city driving. Minis are incredibly compact, and the Mini is the model for most small cars today. In a famous scene from the film *The Italian Job*, one was used to escape from a bank robbery.

In 2000, 25 Austrians got in one Volkswagen Beetle!

! Early windshields were made of ordinary glass.

I didn't know that

dummies test cars. Before they go on the market, new cars are tested for safety with crash test dummies—accurate models of human beings—in crash situations.

Can you find the crash test bear?

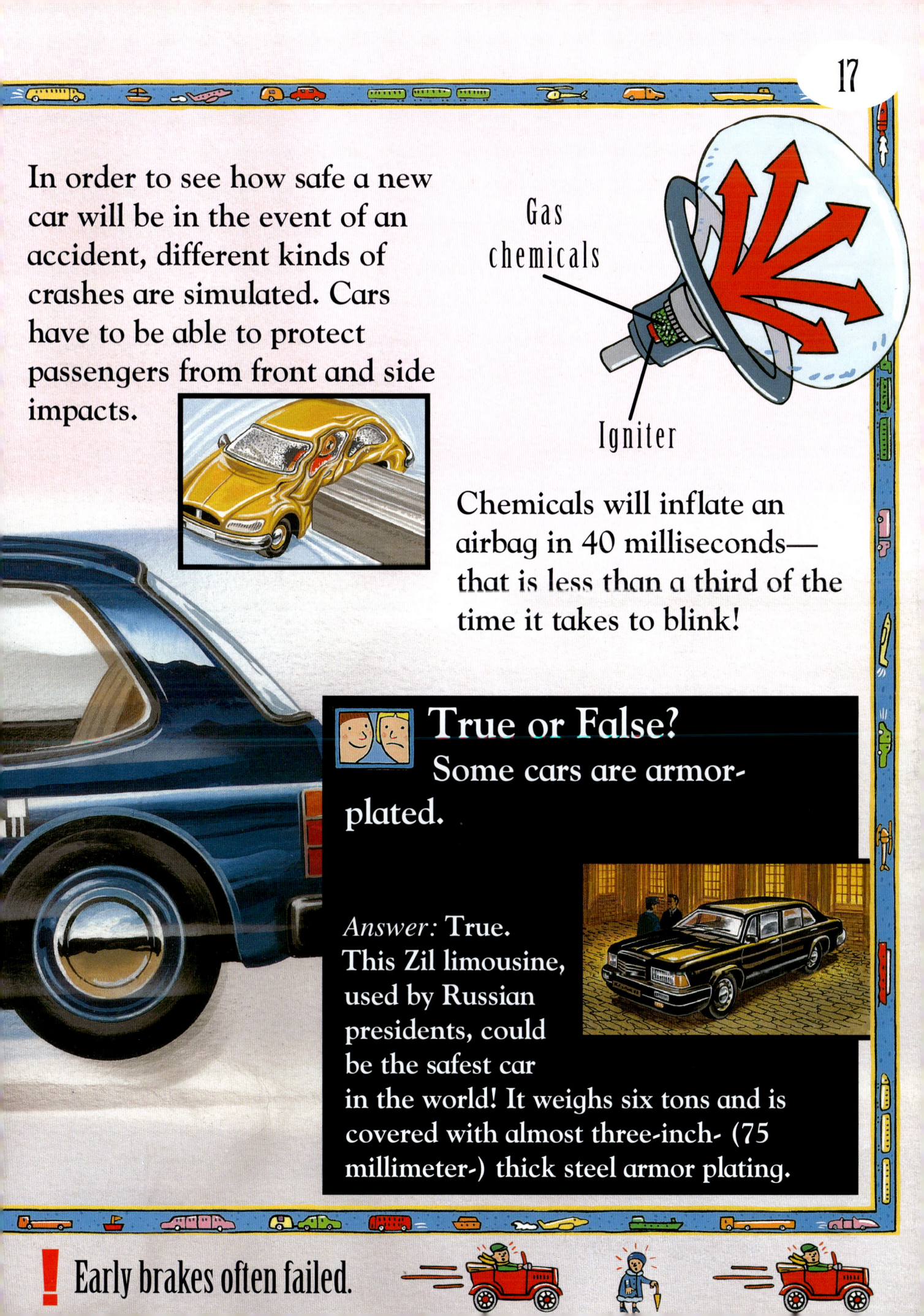

In order to see how safe a new car will be in the event of an accident, different kinds of crashes are simulated. Cars have to be able to protect passengers from front and side impacts.

Gas chemicals

Igniter

Chemicals will inflate an airbag in 40 milliseconds—that is less than a third of the time it takes to blink!

True or False?
Some cars are armor-plated.

Answer: **True.** This Zil limousine, used by Russian presidents, could be the safest car in the world! It weighs six tons and is covered with almost three-inch- (75 millimeter-) thick steel armor plating.

! Early brakes often failed.

! The first Grand Prix race ("big prize" in French) was in France in 1906.

I didn't know that

some cars have wings. Formula One cars, which go up to 208 miles (336 kilometers) per hour, are designed with upside-down wings, which push the car downward. This makes them handle better.

Formula One cars need to have different types of tires for wet, dry, and snowy weather. Sometimes the tires are changed mid-race.

Slick tire

Wet weather tire

Every year, drivers compete in up to 16 Grand Prix races around the world. Each race is at least 186 miles (300 kilometers) long. The most difficult race in is Monaco, where drivers have to negotiate narrow city streets at high speeds.

 **True or False?**
Tires can be changed in less than 10 seconds.

Answer: **True.** When something goes wrong with a car in the middle of a race, the driver pulls into a pit lane. Pit crew mechanics must be able to change tires incredibly quickly.

Driver Juan Fangio won five world championships in seven years.

! The first ever car race was in 1887.

I didn't know that

some cars need parachutes. Dragsters race 400 meters in less than five seconds! By the end, they are going so fast, they need parachutes to slow them down.

Can you find the oil can?

Rally cars race against the clock over bumpy, off-road courses. The cars have specially strengthened suspension. The driver and the navigator, the person who gives directions, are protected by a steel safety cage.

20

In the grueling Le Mans 24 Heures, drivers race for a day without stopping. The race used to begin with drivers running to their cars, but this was abandoned because it was too dangerous.

To see how slowly a parachute will fall when it is filled with air, attach a piece of string to each corner of a bandana. Fasten the ends of the strings to a ball of modeling clay. Throw it high into the air.

! The longest ever rally is from London to Sydney—19,173 miles (30,857 kilometers)!

! When Thrust SCC broke the sound barrier, there was a loud bang.

I didn't know that

a car can go faster than sound. In October 1997, Thrust SCC became the first car to break the sound barrier. In Black Rock, Nevada, it reached an incredible 766.6 miles (1,233.7 kilometers) per hour!

The 223 mph (360km/h) McLaren F-1 is the fastest road car ever. Underneath, it has fans, which "glue" it to the road.

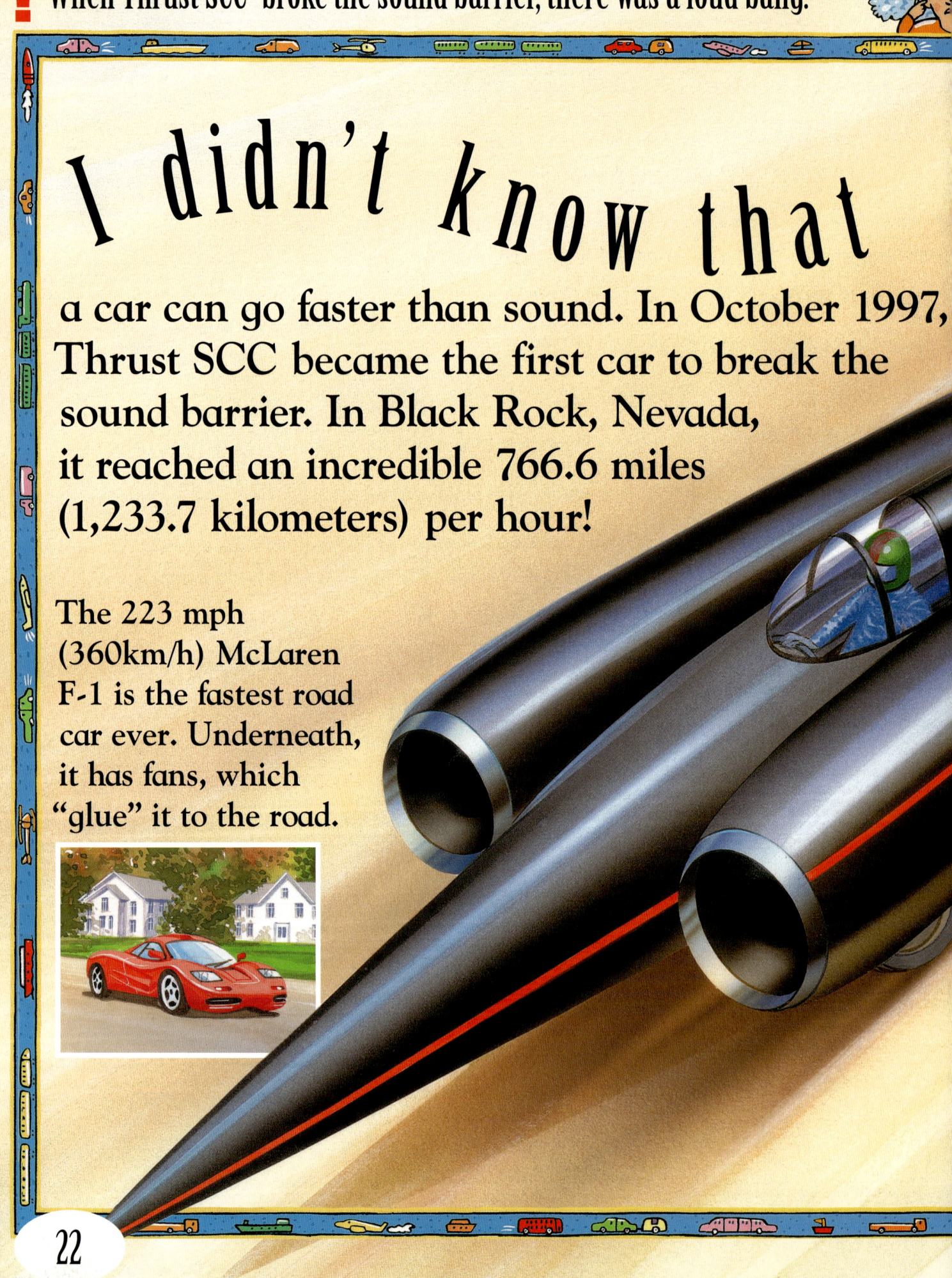

This odd-looking, pancake-shaped Railton Mobil Special was also a record breaker. Driven by John Cobb in 1947, it reached a speed of 394 mph (634 km/h), exceeding the previous record set by the Thunderbolt by 49 mph (78 km/h).

Donald Campbell broke the land-speed record in 1964, reaching speeds of 431 mph (694 km/h) in his gas-powered Bluebird car.

! In 1994, an electric car traveled at 186 mph (300 km/h).

! The Grosser Mercedes, used by the German Army, had six wheels.

I didn't know that

some cars can swim. The Lotus Esprit in the James Bond film *The Spy Who Loved Me* could change into a submarine. Underwater, the wheels turned into propellers.

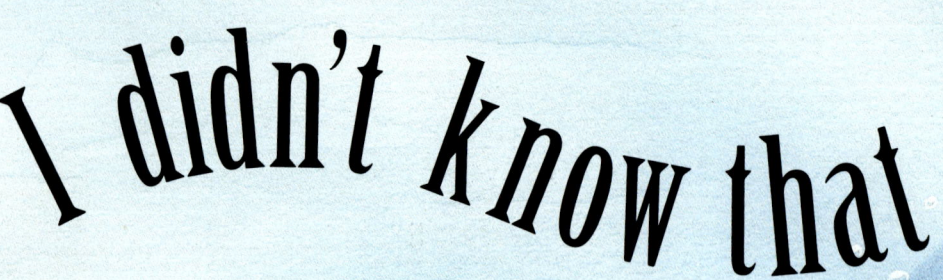

This funny-looking car is the 1923 Leyat Aerocar. It was pulled along by an enormous wooden propeller at up to 99 mph (160 km/h). However, propellers never became popular.

Can you find the starfish?

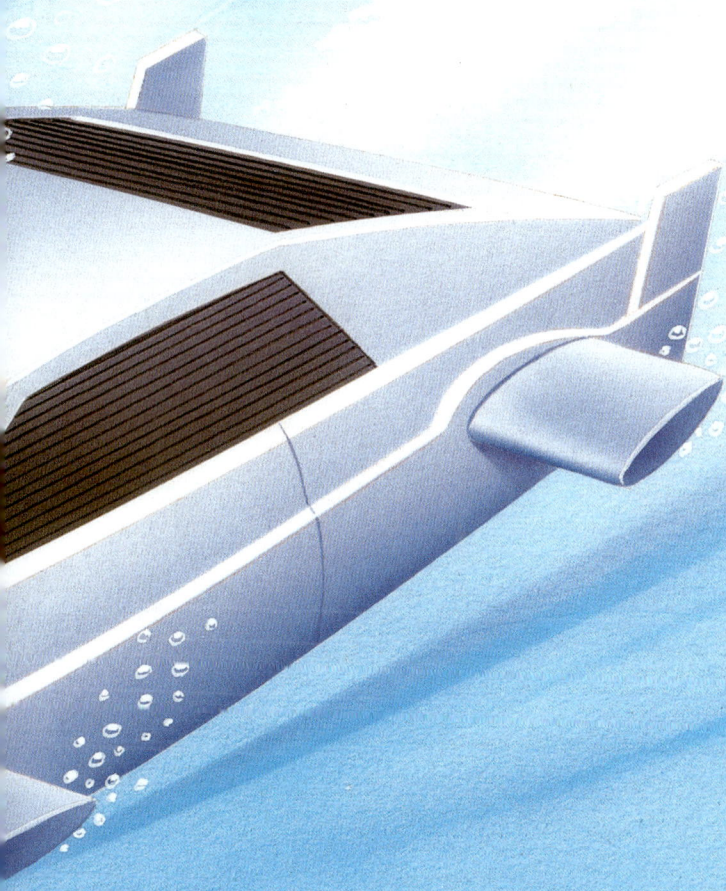

Cars that regularly drive off the road, like the Range Rover, need to have large, grappling wheels and specially strengthened suspension so they don't get stuck in the mud. They can drive over fields and mountains, across ice, and through rivers.

The Bubble car was briefly popular in the 1950s as a small car for city-dwellers. It had a two-cylinder engine, a door at the front, three wheels, and no reverse gear.

! The world's smallest model car is only .026 inches (.67 mm) long.

! 40% of cars in Brazil run on pure alcohol.

I didn't know that

some cars have two engines. The Toyota Prius has an electric engine for starting and low speeds, and a gasoline engine, which kicks in when the car reaches a higher speed.

Can you find three rabbits?

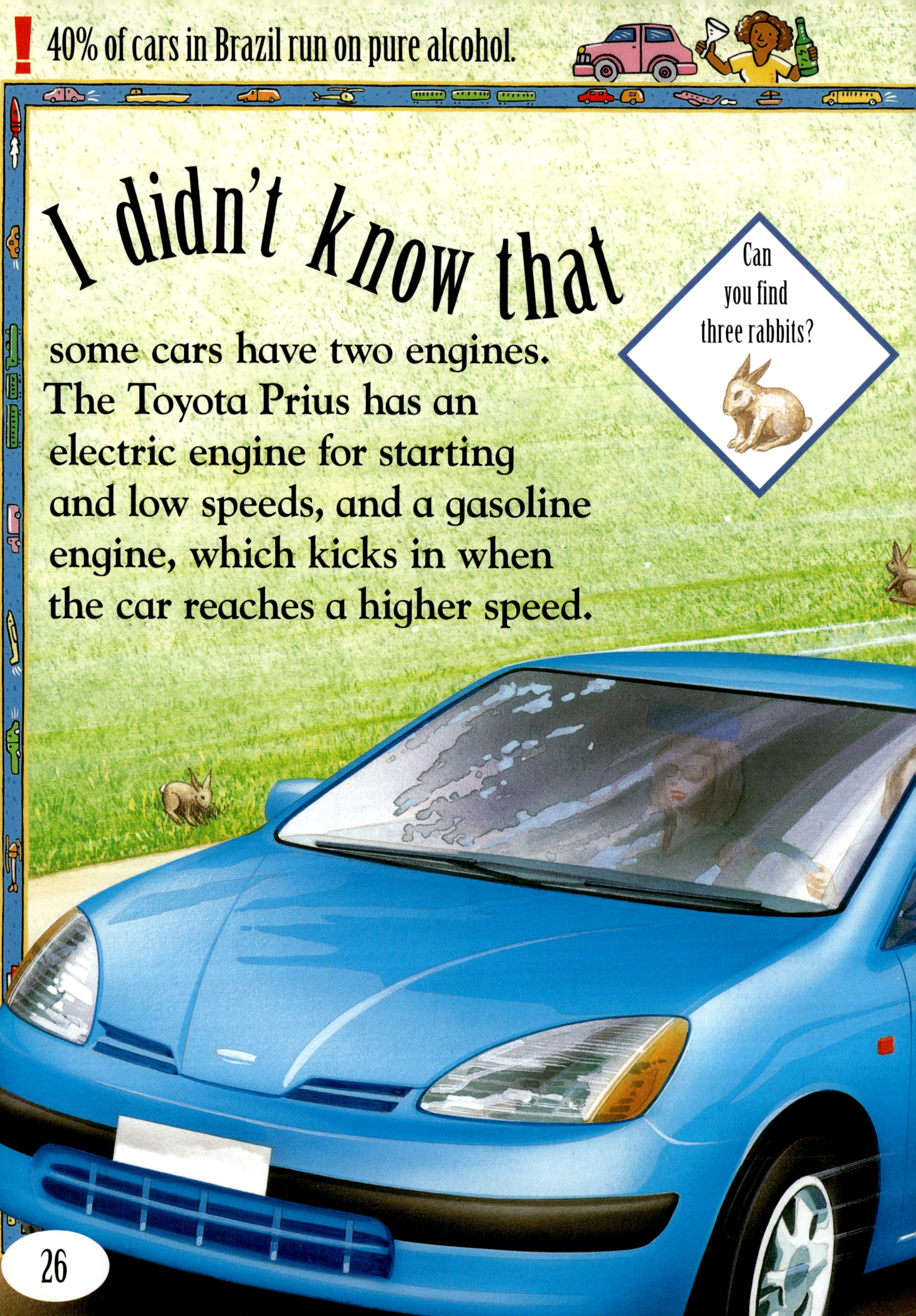

This car has been fitted with a solar panel on the roof, which absorbs heat energy from the sun and converts it into electricity. Cars like this need a hot climate. In Australia, there is a race from Darwin to Adelaide, which is exclusively for solar-powered cars.

Some cars are entirely driven by electric motors, not gasoline engines. They are better for the environment, but they can't go very fast and have to be recharged often.

❗ In 1896, some London taxis were electric powered.

! Future cars might float in mid-air!

I didn't know that

cars in the future will have brains. Cars in the future may be able to think for themselves! They will have a central computer, which will control many of their functions, making them safer and easier to use.

Sensors in the car of the future will be able to detect bumps and potholes in the road ahead, and adjust the suspension accordingly to give the smoothest possible ride.

Using airplane technology, a "head-up display" will project information onto the windshield so that the driver doesn't have to look down at the dashboard. This is much safer, as drivers can concentrate on the road ahead.

On the motorway, computers will be able to measure the distance from the car in front and keep you at a safe distance. You could then drive quickly, but safely.

! In the future, cars might drive themselves.

Glossary

Aerodynamic
A shape, like a modern car, which cuts through air easily.

Airbag
A sack which fills with air when a car hits another object. It protects the driver and passengers from injury.

Electric engine
An engine that is powered by electric energy stored in batteries. Electric engines do not produce waste products like those that burn gas or diesel.

Formula One
The set of rules describing car specifications that Formula One cars have to follow.

Gas engine
An engine that burns gasoline to move a car. Gas engines give off poisonous gases.

Head-up display
The projection of information onto the cockpit of an airplane or the windshield of a car. The drivers can then see it without taking their eyes off where they are going.

Mass-produced
Manufactured on a large scale using machines and people to carry out different parts of the construction process.

Production line
A manufacturing method in which workers are positioned in lines. The work passes from stage to stage.

Solar panel
A device that collects energy from the sun's rays and turns it into electric energy for heating or driving an engine.

Sound barrier
Any vehicle that travels faster than sound waves move through the air (about 1,082 feet, or 330 meters, per second on ground level) is said to have broken the sound barrier.

Suspension
A system of springs or other devices that smooth out the ride of a vehicle.

Road car
A car which is on sale to the public, used for driving on roads instead of in races.

Index

accident 17
aerodynamic 11, 30
airbag 17, 30
armor-plated 17
Auburn Speedster 12

Benz, Karl 7
Benz Motorwagen 6
Bluebird 23
Bordino Steam Carriage 7
bubble car 25
Bugatti Royale 13

Campbell, Donald 23
computers 11, 28, 19
crashes 16, 17

Daimler, Gottlieb 7
dragsters 20
dummies 16

engine 8, 9
electric engine 26, 27, 30

Ford, Henry 11

Ford Model-T 11
Ford Mustang 15
Formula One 18, 9, 30

gas engine 6, 7, 31
Grand Prix 13, 18

head-up display 28, 29, 30

Le Mans 21
Leyat Aerocar 24
Lotus Esprit 24

mass-produced 11, 31
Mercedes W125 13
McLaren F-1 22
Mini 14
motorway 28

Napier Railton 22

parachutes 20, 21
pistons 9
pit crew 19
production line 11, 31
propeller 24

rally cars 20
Range Rover 25
road car 20, 22, 31
Rolls Royce Silver Ghost 12

solar panel 27, 31
sound barrier 23, 31
suspension 25, 29, 31

Thrust SCC 23
Thunderbird 13
tires 19, 25

Volkswagen Beetle 15

wheels 6, 25
wind tunnel 11

32